if this world falls apart

if this world falls apart

poems by
LOU LIPSITZ

LYNX HOUSE PRESS
Spokane, Washington

ACKNOWLEDGEMENTS

Poems in this manuscript have been published in the following journals, sometimes in slightly different form:

The Sun, The Hudson Review, Witness, Solo, Kansas Quarterly, Pembroke Magazine, Southern Poetry Review, The Texas Review, Bellevue Literary Review, Paterson Literary Review, Oberon, Mudfish, The Great River Review, Kakalak 2008, 2009

Cover art: photograph by Lou Lipsitz
Author photo: Fred L. Stephens
Cover & book design: Christine Holbert

FIRST EDITION

Library of Congress Cataloging-in-Publication Data

Lipsitz, Lewis.
If this world falls apart / by Lou Lipsitz.
   p. cm.
ISBN 978-0-89924-121-0 (alk. paper)
1. Postmodernism—Psychological aspects—Poetry. I. Title.
PS3562.I6I4 2011
811'.54—dc22
                              2011009708

For my comrades at the annual North Carolina Men's Gatherings who helped me learn the bravery and exhilaration of sharing my grief and my love, and for George Hitchcock.

TABLE OF CONTENTS

PART 1

AFTER MY GRANDFATHER'S SECOND STROKE

Three week coma: then he woke one day
unable to speak or move his left arm.
But came back, piece by amazing piece—
PT, exercise and after a time it was him again
and we figured the binges would start up.

But instead he stayed in his room all evening
radio on—and let his beard grow out white.

Instead of not coming home for a week,
or coming home cursing five nights in a row,
he was silent. After a few hours he'd emerge
for a snack: bread, jam and tea before bed.

We snuck in one day when he was taking a stroll
and found the poems:
one about the fear of death he experienced before
the coma, one about what an insect feels,
one about walking alone,
one about a woman he could not speak of, one
about the ocean and how it might feel to be
a blind man stepping out into it, not knowing
the size of the waves, one about how he'd seen
his mother's breasts when she was drunk
and wild and he wanted to run into the street.

He'd dug a secret tunnel under our house
leading beyond the lake into the forgotten valley
where they spoke a language of clay and remembrance.

No one mentioned the poems,
but something changed.
My anger began to dissolve.
And when we assembled at the table for dinner
I noticed how my grandmother
who had not slept in the same bed with him
for thirty years, would sometimes,
while serving the food, reach over
to touch his hand.

FISHING WITH MY SON ON LAKE CHAMPLAIN

He's a big guy now, not the boy
who sat with me so many hours
in the sun-flooded rowboat thirty years ago
when, despite my ignorance,
I did my best to act like a fisherman
and show him how.

So much has fallen apart,
the tangled gear rusted with neglect;
so much unsaid, fought over,
yet we can still do this together:
sit near in the way men do;
focus on tackle, bait, lures, lake, winds
and, of course, the elusive fish
we mean to tempt from their murky world.

I see his boyish joy again,
sense the depths that lurk beneath our boat.
Lucky, a northern pike strikes our lure.
We've never seen one before.
Jon brings him in and I hold him firmly
below the head and work the hook out
so we can throw him back.
He's long, fierce looking and beautiful:
square jaw, small sharp teeth,
faint purple markings on his belly.

A visitor from the other world.
Will he heal as in the stories?
Or say, "Get serious. I'm supposed to be eaten."

A long filament of days stretches across the water.
We flick the rod and the reel lets out the line:
almost invisible, knotted here and there,
settling quietly downward. Time's
flickering cocoon.

This man, Werner Aspenstrom, was born
in the country but lived in the big city for years
and was never entirely comfortable anywhere.

That's good. I like that. He went out
into nature, as we call it, the farmland,
thick forests, river valleys where
the torrents of snowmelt roar along.
He saw the black butterfly
with orange stripes on its wings alight
on a pile of deer droppings.
He noticed the spot of sunshine
that edged its way into a clearing
among the great fir trees. Some people
say such things help to heal us.

The Swedish poet is not so sure. I like that.
Ok, he says, this helps a little. We quiet down.
And a poem can help too, insinuating itself
into our chaotic and bewildered psyches
like a tiny man we make out on a distant hillside
waving his arms. He wears a bright blue shirt.
Is he signaling us to stop, to come over?

We begin to drive in his direction, but then
we lose sight of him and realize
we have to get back soon. We don't
have time to keep looking. It's
starting to snow. The tunnel's
coming up; the glare of those headlights. Our
own headlights racing toward us from the future.

THE QUESTION

My mother at eighty-six
has raised a question.
      It's occurred to her
that my father
      forty-five years ago
spent too many Saturdays
at work.

My mother, who wept
quite briefly
after her husband
      collapsed
      in the bathroom and
died of a coronary;
      who remarried
within a year and had
the time of her life
      taking cruises
that my father
could never have afforded;
who has rarely spoken
      of him for years;
is now starting
      to wonder: was he
really working
      all those Saturdays?

Now, in the quiet of the big apartment,
second husband also gone,
      her mind wanders back;
she remembers

a woman who phoned once
        started to ask
for Jack
        and suddenly hung up.
And this is when
she calls me
        and asks if I know
the answer.

And of course I do.
        I, the secret-keeper,
who has found his way out
        of every embrace—

I know her phone number,
the way to her apartment,
her body in a black kimono
        as she answers the door.

From time to time
        he slept with one who had
        what he called "real class,"
who knew how to dress.
Maybe she'd spent time
in Europe
        and developed a taste for luxury.
She worked for some specialty store
and would watch coolly
as my father—
        stylish, darkly Mediterranean,
        recently manicured,
        the sleeves of his shirt
rolled up on his forearms,
colorful tie loosened—
        showed her the latest in sportswear.
And then
        asked her to dinner,
        business of course (though
she understood).
        A sleek brunette, maybe,
with great legs.
        Next day, he'd send flowers
and a romantic note.
"Women," he told me,
        "crave attention."

From time to time, it
was a prostitute.
        Nothing tawdry,
not the tough whores he

and his buddies used to drive
up to Albany for
when they were eighteen.
        Nothing extravagant
either. A small, neat West Side
apartment. Curtains in the bedroom
like home. She'd never
make him rush. He could take
        the full hour if he wanted to.
"They're the only
ones," he told me, "who really know
how to please a man."

But mostly, the women
were like him,
        Jews or Italians out
of Brooklyn or the Bronx, one step
from the ethnic ghettos, trying
        not to smell of pastrami
or spaghetti sauce, or talk
with an accent;
        dressed to kill, slick and ready
with a joke—good-looking, youthful
women who glanced in the mirror
        a lot and wore
fashionable clothes;
        were determined above all
        not to be old-fashioned;
who'd discovered quickly
        what marriage could offer,
and what it couldn't; who could
keep their mouths shut
        and not tell other people
        what they didn't need
to know anyway.

They liked to gamble, but
not too heavily.

The way I imagine it,
        only once in twenty-five years
did any woman come close.
        He was nearing fifty
and watching the gray make its steady advances
        like a disorganized guerilla army
through the countryside
        of his thinning hair.

She was fifteen years younger
from a department store in some
        small midwestern
town, and something
        about her shyness
cut way into him.
        They had sex twice, but he was
haunted. She never asked
for anything,
        and he was afraid he
couldn't forget her.
        He knew what it would mean
if this ever got out—
        what would happen to the family,
        what his sisters would say.
He wasn't someone
        to throw it all away
        on one spin of the wheel.
So he let it die out: watching TV, tossing
        the football with me
in the street.

Somewhere in his mid-fifties
he got friendly with a seamstress
        who worked in his shop—
        a motherly woman
with a sick husband.
They worked late.
and she made him dinner
        He gave her extra money,
quietly, just relaxed and
let it happen.
        Only his wife couldn't
see it. She was fond of saying
over and over:
        "Jack worships
the ground I walk on."

Sundays, twice a year, he and I
went to the cemetery where
        his father was buried.
We mumbled the
Hebrew prayer for the dead and,
        keeping with tradition,
put a small rock on the gravestone
to show we'd come.
        Usually, we went home
without a word,
but once, when I was twenty,
        I saw him wipe away tears,
and he started to talk about
my grandfather:
        "He was the sweetest guy.
Everybody loved him. But I'd hear
my mother yelling at him
in the back room.
        And he never yelled back.

Because everything
        she said was true:
        he ran around and gambled
and . . ." He stopped.
        "Just once
I wanted to hear him
yell back at her:
        'Yes, I'm foolish, but
you don't know me and you
never will.'"

Twenty-five feet to
the ceiling
of the gym

junior high school, P.S. 232
and in one corner
      two ropes
      —rough, hand-burning, dark-yellow ropes,
      the test of our guts
(supposedly)

      Climb all the way up
or you don't graduate -
      you stay back until
you can do it, they said.
      I wasn't the only one
who believed them.

No one taught us.
      Sure, they showed
us once:

      Pull with your
arms like this and
      wrap the rope
around your leg, get a grip
between your
sneakers.

      whenever I could
get up the nerve
when no one

   was looking
I tried to practice—
    never making it more
      than ten feet before my
12-year-old skinny-boy
    arms
failed
    and I hung there,
legs thrashing.

But on the appointed day
    in June
adrenaline pounding, fear
    doing its powerful work,
I heard my name called and
    like a hunted animal
I leaped forward and before
    I could register what was
happening
    the boy who inhabited me
went up that rope
    arms alone pulling him
    the entire way, which
I had thought
    impossible.

And then
    that strange moment at the top,
looking down
    twenty-five feet,
elated and dazed, my altered state
    just beginning to recede,
twenty-five feet to fall, or slide,
    or descend in triumph;
such a long way down

and I was even more afraid
—all those years in front of me
and me
not knowing any better how
to return to earth
than I'd known how to ascend.
The teacher yelling: You
can't stay up there
all day, for chrissake.
my arms starting
to seriously ache
the fear
of falling
but also
a wish
to leap into the air
and discover what might happen—
it was only life
after all
and I could
glimpse
below me
the rushing water
the rocks
and the girl
among
the burning flowers.

AFTER A DREAM

In the night I spoke of my father again
how he died so suddenly.

In the night I saw my children leaving
as they had to.

I saw my son and went to him slowly
not knowing how he regarded me
and hugged him and wept.

So much had happened
I was so unprepared.

I stood among the dark angles of my life
unable to grasp where I was.

And then I saw through
into the shattered
treasure house of another day.

WHY BASEBALL DOESN'T MATTER

It's not because the game's so slow,
that the pitcher has to step down off the mound,
pick up the resin bag, adjust his hat, adjust
his pants, spit, pound his glove,
step back onto the rubber,
then peer down, get the sign
nod approval and only then rear back,
and unleash the baseball.

It's not that basketball has more action:
the gliding down court—dragonflies in a mating dance.
Start then stop, backtrack, fake,
then dart toward the basket.

Nor that football has that heavy military vibe,
with the tanks moving into position,
the "bomb" lofted downfield, and the
grim drama of the goal line stand
some beachhead, Iwo Jima,
young men pinned down in the mud.

And it's not that America's altogether
changed (though it has.) It's not
the steroid home runs, not
those million dollar player salaries,
not the glitzy gold chains
around their expensive necks.
not the greedy owners, not that the Dodgers
left Brooklyn and the Braves left Boston or
the . . . what was it . . . left where?

It's that tonight, in midsummer,
under an inquisitive fraction of a moon,
the wind pulls a thin blanket of dust
off the distant fields and carries it for miles.

I feel the black edges of night
like a curled fern leaf about to unfold,
and a small grasshopper
settles on my hand and I lift it and
watch it, suddenly, fly from me
like a knuckle ball, like the startling,
crooked spirit of grief.

And I stand up and look around
and find myself alone
for the long seventh inning stretch,
tiny night lights appearing inevitably
over this mysterious, damaged world
of triumphs.

> By midlife we suffer the growing split between
> the acquired personality and the natural self.
>
> —James Hollis, *Under Saturn's Shadow*

> . . . an old woman put her hand to her brow and
> exclaimed . . . "It is Rip Van Winkle . . . Where have
> you been this twenty years?"
>
> —Washington Irving

Deep in the forest, he turned slightly
and brushed against a stone. As if in the distance,
he smelled the rotted maple leaves
that had covered him so long. Then
he felt a gnawing hunger, reached down
to touch his once ample belly
and in a moment of terror and confusion
realized he was thin as a skeleton!

Flinging leaves away, he stumbled back down
the mountain remembering the band of celebrants,
dressed in costumes from some psychedelic
fairy tale and the brown concoction
he'd drunk for "psychic rejuvenation."

Reentering the village, his voice failed.
The inhabitants stood back at first, fearing
he was a troll. Led to his former home,
there was his wife, matronly now
and even more stern. He knew immediately
that shrewish woman held him in bonds no more
and danced two wild minutes, then fell in a heap.

It took a good while for him to recover.
A new entrepreneur at the real estate company
saw his potential and described Rip as
"the perfect salesman for mountain land ."
But Rip had no interest in selling anything.

He chose to live outdoors, day after day,
painting in watercolors the vivid forms
stored in his psyche those twenty years:
fantastic creatures, human shapes
with hooves for eyes
and haggard faces for hands.
His most admired creation was a beautiful woman
with blazing red hair and the hind legs of an ox.
He explained that she had been his lover,
who had visited during his epic sleep and
was sometimes with him still.

On evening walks through the woods
middle-aged men accompanied him.
He encouraged them to write poems,
sit quietly and study their dreams.
As for the beautiful woman,
he told them she was a mystery
he would never unravel.

Certain nights, as the seasons changed,
Rip chanted and prayed at the graveyard.
His odd trembling dance reminded some
of a captain on deck in a storm,
swaying as the boat tossed,
eyes closed, hands gripping the wheel;
but to others, he seemed a ghost
knocking, over and over, at the door of a house
closed to him forever.

IF THIS WORLD FALLS APART

for Bennett

I never troubled to grasp the basic principles
of how my voice zings through the phone lines
and into your ear; and so, the phones out,
I could not even begin to get a handle on how
to recreate the way I could call to ask you
if this world had truly fallen apart, or
if this was another serious but passing crisis.

And the roads blocked by shattered trees,
I would have to walk over and ask you
and see what you thought.
That would take most of the day.
So I'd have to stay the night
and have supper at your house,
though I'm not sure how we would cook
without any power or light.
Fire, most likely, or eat cold out of the garden.

Millennia of human struggle and invention
would be lost if it depended on us—
two clueless poets collecting sticks
along a dark road;
men of lifelong impracticality,
depending on others to do
the functional things that repair our intricate
systems.

Although, on the other hand, there would be the dance
you would certainly do at sunset to lift our spirits.

And to accompany you, I would find
a hollow reed and put my fingers
over the holes I'd burned through it
and begin to blow.

> And the Lord God planted a garden in Eden,
> in the east; and there he put the man whom he
> had formed. And out of the ground the Lord God
> made to grow every tree that is pleasant to the
> sight and good for food.
>
> *—Genesis 2: 8-9*

From the beginning we were naked here
and had to discover ways of keeping warm.

With stealth, we crossed the great savannas
chasing after game with spears and sharpened stones,
learning to take shelter from the wind-dust.

We made only crude sounds, shouting
of danger, running and signaling with our arms.
And we had to kill, always, just to go on living.
We took the meat and skins and some of us
were ripped apart in those huge jaws.
Otherwise, we would not be as we are—
fierce, clever, clannish, untrusting.

I'm not saying that all the old story
was deception. We found dark plums,
apples, herds moving, creeping things.
We discovered seeds and the eggs
of tortoises from the sea.
But often we were shaken by sky-filling storms.
We fell sick in ways we could not cure.
Dark moods came over us.

Often we became lost
and stumbled back at night
to sit by the fire where
we could imagine great stories.
We searched for The Garden, but never found it.

We continue to believe there must be
another way. Sometimes in dreams
we get a glimpse of it, a path,
some light, a hand that shaped us.
But there is actually only one place
where everything is given, where
we are held in warmth and shadows,
our tiny mouths pushed against her
the milk obliging our tongues.

WATCHING THE TV VERSION OF THE HOLOCAUST

Just when the mother
was being shoved with the rest
toward the cattle car bound for Auschwitz
and her daughter grabbed for the sleeve of her coat,
just as the son who had joined
the Czech partisans was about to kill
for the first time—
another young boy in Nazi uniform,
shoot him in the face with a submachine gun—
the family in their large, brightly lit
bathroom started quarreling about toothpastes.

Just as the mother and father noticed
the strange smelling smoke and cinders.
as the artist son was tortured,
and his wife had to fuck the prison guard
to get messages to her husband;
the gleeful woman told us
we could get rid of stains and odors
making sure nothing stuck
to the inside of the dryer.

REGRET

> the traveler armed with sterile resistances . . .
>
> —*Pablo Neruda*

The beggar with the stripped gray sack
follows me around,
but he won't take the money I offer.

When I go into the restaurant
he stands outside
cap in hand
waiting for others to offer help.

I drink two glasses of decent wine
and, with you, laugh for a time
about life's stupidities, how
we're getting older, how
things are harder than we thought,
how the children forget about us,
etc. . . .

Then later I see him, coat collar
turned up against the cold,
face roughened by the wind,
milky eyes a sign of some disease.

I will think of him just before I get to sleep.
And if I get up and go to the window
he will be there sometimes,
across the street, wrapped in his blanket
at the entrance to the alley.

He's waiting for me to join him;
to take the long, silent journey into the dried leaf,
o, autumn, o soul!

MAGNETIC RESONANCE IMAGING

for Diane and Paul

> We are here to awaken from the illusion
> of our separateness.
>
> *—Thich Nhat Hanh*

I lay inside the MRI, claustrophobic tube,
its surface a few inches from my face;
my body entirely surrounded
by the smooth metal cylinder that held me
not like a bean in a pod,
but—as one inevitably thinks—
the body, one day, in its plain box in the earth.

And I felt the strange transitoriness of all things.
I tried becoming a quick Buddhist
because Diane reminded me to breathe and let go.
I closed my eyes and saw you, Paul,
and your teacher. You walked in a garden
and I heard his sparkling, gentle voice.
He spoke of chewing the brown rice
slowly, tasting the earthy nectar of each grain.

Then I went far back into myself
and saw us in your living room,
forty-five years ago—
before I knew about the body's failures;
before you knew the grim endings
it would be your lot to endure—

I realized I could never practice true
nonattachment. I would love too many things
for too long.
The careful machine whirred on,
searching for the disorder.

> About suffering, they were never wrong,
> The Old Masters.

—W.H. Auden, *Musee des Beaux Arts*

They showed us that people don't notice, or care
or want to know.

Forty windows close when the desperate girl
screams in the alley. Cars zoom by the strange man
staggering alongside the road.

Brueghel put the evidence in his famous painting:
the boy Icarus disappears into the sea,
amazing wings useless as he falls, making
a tiny splash.

Yet the ploughman in the foreground
goes on ploughing. Vacationers
on a pleasure ship, startled for a moment
to see him disappearing, disbelieve
what they saw and turn away
to go to dinner.

But here is my question: where is the father
in this painting? Where is Daedalus,
who conceived and created the wings
and planned their escape from the island prison;
who carefully instructed his son on the dangers
of flight and then, magically, rose
into the air with him?

Like visionary beings they floated
on wind currents. All day they flew
playful and triumphant. But
toward evening
when Daedalus glanced back
his son was gone.

He scanned the waters for
a sign of his foolish, elated boy;
and not finding Icarus,

searched across every island and finally,
realizing what must have happened;
seeing the tire marks, pulled up
to the spot, saw the wreck still smoldering,
and ran into the ditch, choking
back his tears, frantically trying to pry
open the door
of the crushed vehicle.

THE COUPLE

for Ben, 1885-1972
for Sadie, 1888-1971

They died just months apart, made
twins by the desolate voyage, mariners
without a port, exiles together -
one pulled down into the end and then
the other, tethered as they were
to their damaged vessel, still somehow
afloat, barely, masts long-ago broken,
sails torn apart, something strange, slow
and powerful wearing away
even the dark polished oak, once thick
as elephant legs. And what they had left
was a leak-infested raft of a thing,
remnant, unsteerable, creature of tides
and storms. They roped themselves
to the hooks and rings that remained,
letting whatever prevailed take them,
surrendering to that fate, wasting, salt-encrusted.

Sixty-five years together in the silence.
Silence, silence, silence and the casual
passage of broken time.

The rabbi placed his hands on each
of their heads and spoke a blessing. She,
the young redheaded immigrant, speaking
Hungarian, kosher, saying her prayers,
sweet faced, ambitious and afraid; and he,
the native-born poorboy, finding money

however; drinking, loving the racetrack
and the splendor of horses, singing
with the Irish in their bars. He fell in love
with her green eyes. Oceans, weren't they?

WEAVER DAIRY ROAD

There's a shopping center now
and medical offices; two upscale
subdivisions hidden behind
smooth cream-colored concrete walls
that ride to the peak of the hill.
There's the art theatre now we always
wished for back then when this road
was woods mainly
and a few small houses
tucked back from sight.

But despite all that, the pines, oaks
and sweet gum on the north side of the road,
where we used to make love,
haven't been cleared yet.
There's still that rutted old farm path
where you used to pull
the station wagon in—a dark green
vehicle hidden in the uproar
blossomings of April.

I'd take my shirt off, showing the
skinny soul I'd hidden underneath—
my big head full of academic ideas,
and stand unproudly as you
grabbed the blanket out of the back
and lay yourself down, pulling up
your colorful loose dress, slipping
off your panties.

We were always hurried.
You had sons to get back to. I had
my job. We had no idea what
we were doing. Only
that this had changed
everything.

How many times did we
lie down on the unsoft earth
and join our bodies?
Never enough.

Your flushed face mixed
with reddish dirt, dogwood
blossoms and the smell
of our juices on the pine needle
ground.

Today, driving the hill
I saw the new high school
and remembered how you
were my school then—
those learnings so brief
and exquisite
that still make me weep.

Old love, old love,
tender, careless alphabet,
wild parabola,
page of the wisdom book
turned to ash
by the welder's arc
of our rapturous hands.

PART 2

Those words that cannot be heard all day,
barely imagined:
hidden in the bushes, in children's games,
diving off a ledge into the quarry
hitting their heads never to resurface.
They might fall from the tree like a nut
and root in the earth; lurk around the corner,
some snake or accident,
ready to make your life jump,
or drift and cling like dust
floating in your kitchen.
They could disappear like the fishing boat
you knew was coming through the fog,
or maybe in a dream someone will shout,
but you can't hear it.

You are just not ready.
Still, they will come toward you at night.
You'll feel them in the room
surrounding you: inexplicable, alien presences.
They might tap you with their insistent fingers
and you'll sit up and look around, trembling.

An old song could come to you then.
You don't know why. The Hungarian midwife
hums it as she washes her hands.
Then she turns to you.

And here is the fact: you are giving birth.
It's unclear how or when, but your life slowly,
bloodily, is being pushed out
into your own hands.

VACATION

How many days before
the in comes out?

I can verify that there are buds on your elbows
and some odd looking bumps
on the branches of your shoulder blades

I see the little vine
that edged out of your brain
snaking around your left ear

You're crying now—the way
a tree might sob, just
standing there, shaking, unable to escape.

Is it the raw, unending poetry
that vibrates through the roots of the day,
or the undefinable, ravishing music
of the night?

How great it is to weep, really,
and degenerate into a creature
with no will of its own! That
grows from a seed and stands still
rooted right there.

So much time
to transform and transform.
To decay! Such great work!

Because all the instruments
don't agree

because there is too much
song, somewhere,
waiting and

I cannot breathe it

because when the mandolin
begins its grasshopper leaping
          and the piano's bruised ankles
ache
          and the guitar opens itself
like a wren fluttering inside
its nest

          I am still too silent
humming, walking,
unable to begin my devotions.

NOW, AFTER SO MANY DAYS

for a therapist

Now, after so many days drenched
with confusion, racing past me
like rain-soaked commuters hurrying
to catch the last train home;
and after so many nights alone,
awake, considering what i cannot
ever know again, my dissatisfied heart
yearning to continue its search,
twisting this way and that, flapping
like a windblown flag, and my body,
longing only to renew itself,
quietly, in the darkness where it
begins to forget;
now i come into the room where
i have not known how to work and find
three long hours waiting: the sunlight,
the vast heavy sadness i knew would
call to me. and in my gratitude i begin
to weep, and then, wiping my tears,
sit down to write these lines, to
tell you of this, the strange aching freedom.

VARIATIONS ON A LINE BY
WILLIAM CARLOS WILLIAMS

*Saxifrage is my flower that splits
the rocks.*

1

Ah, how fine to discover
this plant
       —leaves so delicate—
that happens as well
to be a rock splitter.

I remember Yeats warned that
       the heart (under
some fierce conditions) can
become a stone.
And I've encountered foot-thick walls
mortared into place in those middle ages—

       So let's locate Williams' flower
that unfolds and cannot be resisted—
help it grow and
       burst everything open.

We can search night
after night
       —dream after obscure dream.

2

You say this flower splits the rocks?
Actually wedges in
and cracks them apart?

No. In sad truth, it cannot,
but it can "slip through"
            the way the dream
finds its way into the prison
of the self and
            says: "Here's the way out.
                        You don't have to stay."

And you turn then
and grasp
            so clearly
the shadowy turmoil
you were sure
you had to solve:

convicts, prison guards, steel doors,
homemade shivs, towers and machine guns,
and behind it all
the shadowy condemning
judge.

Your drama.

"Here ," the voice whispers,
            "let's split."

3
We were walking
in the garden and I said
"I cannot grow anything these days.

—the soil is too rocky—
            roots
can't locate
a way to hold."

Come over here, she said,
This soil needs
      something.
      let's dig and overturn the earth,
give it air, soften.

      And so she lay down,
opening herself,
wet with liberty.

4
      Eden. Ah, that did not
last, did it?

Obedience way
      too difficult.

Have you noticed
something in us wants
to say "No!"
      grab two handfuls of dirt
          and throw them.

Of course, we are just
      three years old at the time.

But how old were
      Adam and Eve do you
suppose—
          sixteen?

A set up.
The last Act written
      before it ever began.
      Of course Adam's

roused up prick was
serpentine—
        full of earthbound,
crackling knowledge.

We've felt that
        groovy wiggle!

Please—
        let's forgive them.

Better—
        let's honor them
the ancient, disobedient,
erotic ones.

Let's dress their heads
in apple blossoms.
        Kiss them.

They need blessing.

Let's give them the
saxifrage plant.

        They'll carry it out of the Garden
as they wander
        where the Master of Shame
has sent them:
        long shadowy way
of sharp stones.

5

Let's leave the Garden
  with its sad untouchable
tree
  its lonely Right and Wrongness.

Leave the apple half eaten
to rot
  on sacred ground.

There's a word forming
  in the murky underground rivers
you must forage through.

Listen. It drifts upward
among the rocks.

Listen. Green, it
  edges through the cracks, splits
our hearts.

  O brokenhearted race—
take these hope-filled roots—
carry them carefully
  in your dreaming hands.

ELEGY FOR CORSO AND SO MUCH ELSE

Gregory Corso, 1930-2001

Mrs. Lombardi's month-old son is dead
. . . wow, such a small coffin!
And ten black cadillacs to haul it in.

—Corso, *Italian Extravaganza*

i remember the first time i saw you
at the standingroomonly studentshangingoutthewindows poetry
reading
in some big hall yale new haven, 1959,
when crazy stuff like that really did not happen—
not yet—when decorum prevailed
and we were waiting and didn't know it.
ginsberg there, on the edge of the stage, legs dangling,
ringing Tibetan finger cymbals
(we'd never seen before);
paying no attention, everyone guessing
what was supposed to happen next.

and you came striding down center aisle,
yelling words we couldn't make out,
an intruder deciding it's time to have his say;
italian curls and big, startling black eyes,
a crazy man for sure. but no,
it was the other poet, and you climbed on stage,
goony and boyish, laughing, probably stoned
and read to us from a bunch of crumpled-up pages
you took out of your pocket
and from that little red and white text GASOLINE.

strange damn poems—funny, odd, off the map we
had been taught to follow, some other territory.
or maybe it was you yourself
and not the poems. you, so unlike
the poets we'd studied; too zany, too close to us, too
flawed and coarse, too much strange delight,
or, maybe the sense of some
approaching wildness we couldn't grasp,
a confused ecstasy, a decade unscheduled,
disasters waiting, heroin they tried to pry
from your endless hand,
and the "being-torn-apart-haunted-with-meanings,"
searching for the beautiful worlds.

and now new century, swifter than delight, meanings
sogged out, beaten by information,
and he's gone, the black-eyed boy,
Mrs. Corso's kid—
                    Wow!
                              we're a memory.

DR. ZHIVAGO'S DESIRE

Far into the Urals, surrounded by winter,
snowdrifts piled against the house
like mistakes of all the dead generations,
a pack of wolves howling at the edge of the wood,
the Revolution grinding on, engraving
its utopian calendar with blood—
here Zhivago opens the portfolio
and finds his way back to the last poem.

The doctor writes at night,
feeling the cold through his coat and gloves,
barely able to hold the pen in his freezing fingers;
writing the anguished poetry of a man
with two women to love: one, Lara, so distant,
lost among battlefields and destinies;
and the other, his wife, asleep with their children
in the dark satchel of the house.

Tonight Zhivago searches for words the way
a surgeon probes for bullet fragments—
poetry's dark knife penetrating muscle
and shattered bone.
But sometimes words race from him,
escape in all directions, a Moscow crowd
caught in the crossfire—and he writes frantically
until a wolf howls, he looks up, shudders,
then returns to the operating room of
the poem, trying to retrieve what he can,
the gentle doctor's way, bandages of time and
concentration wrapped around the wounds.
Late, he writes of Lara, his foraging heart
prowling the solitude.

Finally, exhausted, the poem unfinished,
he sleeps, head on his desk by the frozen window,
and dreams he's lost in the forest.

Snow has fallen for hours,
In the distance, echoes of artillery.
His body grows numb.
Finally, he lies down on the wet earth,

giving up. It's then she appears, Lara,
who departs and returns,
carrying the great yearning
the way a river carries the bodies of the dead.
Zhivago struggles to his feet and
runs after her, howling like a wolf,
his voice echoing—the longing of the poem
extending its reach—each word a year,
each line the dark ax blade
cutting through a limb.

SOLOMON'S MISTAKE

> And the King said, 'Bring me a sword.' So a
> sword was brought before the King. And the
> King said 'Divide the child in two, and give half
> to the one and half to the other.'
>
> —*1 Kings 3:24-25*

1

The story of King Solomon and his brilliant solution
to the competing claims of the two mothers
is propaganda.

Solomon was busy that day with matters of state
and a long list of supplicants.
Plus, his middle-aged depression
had grown more severe.

He tried listening to the rival claimants,
each tugging on the infant's blanket—
their multiple bracelets echoing in the throne room.
They sounded like lying harlots to him.

Wishing to be through with it, he sent them out
to procure lawyers and dig up the proper documents
he knew did not exist.
It was only outside in the courtyard,
as they went on shrieking,
that a soldier threatened to solve the problem
by cutting the child in half.
And then the true mother stopped him,
offering to give up her claim,
while the other, cunningly, just waited.

And so she, the deceiver, was the one
who received the baby that day
and raised it as her own.

2

Years later, when he was older
and considerably more tranquil,
Solomon had the habit of strolling out among his people;
and one day encountered the real mother
and asked about the child
and the dilemma presented to him years before.

And so he heard the story of the angry soldier
and the threat. How she had given up the child.

And it was then, as she wept,
that Solomon realized what he could have done
so many years before to reveal the truth.

In a flash of despair, he discovered this wisdom—
not the effortless solution mythologized
by those who prefer the idolatry of kings.

HAVE A ＿＿＿ DAY

Have a nice day. Have a memorable day.
Have (however unlikely) a life-changing day.
Have a day of soaking rain and lightning.
Have a confused day thinking about fate.

Have a day of wholes.
Have a day of poorly marked,
unrecognizable wholes you
cannot fathom.
Have a ferocious day, a bleak
unbearable day. Have a
riotously unproductive day;
a grim jaw-clenched, Clint Eastwood vengeful
law enforcement day.
Have a day of raging, hair-yanking
jealousy and meanness. Have a day
of almost grasping
how whole you are; a finely tuned,
empty day.

Have a nice day of walking and circling;
a day of stalking and hunting,
of planting strange seeds and wandering in the woods.
Have a day of endearing nonsense,
of hopelessly combing your hair,
a day of yielding, of swallowing
hard, breathing more deeply,
a day of fondness for beetles
and macabre spectacles, of irreverence
about anything you want, of just
sitting and wondering.

Have a day of wondering if it's
going to help, or if it just doesn't matter;
a day of dark winds
and torrents flowing through the valley,
of diving into cool water
and gasping for breath,
a day of sudden hunger for communion.

Have a day when the crusts you each
were given are lost and you stumble
with your fellows
searching endlessly together.

READING POETRY TO NINETY MEN

—*for John Miller*

> This was the great surprise. There was a forest of
> emotional, imaginal life that modern men were just
> waiting to enter.
>
> —*Michael Meade*

We've been together for two days
descending into an unfamiliar realm.
We're not the same group
that came Friday night with our sleeping bags
to be among so many unknown men.

Now I see my colleague Amnon
struggling with tears.
He's not the only one.
Long withheld, the grief rises, subsides,
and engulfs us.

The first night a grim-faced man
brought a medieval broadsword
to our altar.
He'd been, he said, a "destructive warrior."

Tonight, in a whisper,
he stood before the group again
and offered that sword
to the one man he said he had feared
all weekend—
        a gentle, long-haired singer
—almost a boy

who received the sword with tears—
astonished as the rest of us.
Discovery of our shamed feeling!
that sweeps over and frees us.
Not archeology,
but the living tribe.

Ancient rhythms thump psyche's drum.
Wistful, searching notes flow
through body's tender flute.

I've been asked to read a few poems.
It's time. I open my book
and choose a poem about a jazz clarinetist—
so poor his teeth crumbled,
his instrument broke, for years he couldn't play,
but then, with help, he started again
the music startling and vital.

And suddenly I realize
I'm talking about myself, my own grief.
I look out and see Amnon in the second row
tears on his cheeks
and I can't read another line.

My sudden brothers surround me.
I lower my head
and find I no longer wish to hold back.

BRAILLE

for Jeff, 1941-2004

Time, the punch line to God's favorite joke,
one we never really get.

—Sy Safransky

Retinitis pigmentosa is an eye disease in which there
is damage to the retina. The damage gets worse over time.
There is no effective treatment for this condition.

1

One of your old students called last night.
He'd just heard and wanted to talk.
By the end of the conversation
we were saying we loved each other.
We'd never thought to say that long ago
when we'd felt it and were embarrassed by it.
Now that we're older, losses, life's torturers,
loosen our tongues.

I could say death brings love out,
the way the hounds root out the fox.
I could say that, but we both know
love is the grass the horses trample down
and piss on. The fox is our amazing,
confused intelligence that in this moment
can do nothing but dig deeper
into the dark.

2

So, dear friend, for you, no more struggles,
no more retinitus pigmentosa—
eyesight ebbing away as if a wire screen,
you said, grew thicker, blocking out the light—
no more bumping into objects, bruising
your shins on your way to the kitchen
for a midnight snack; no more hand on my shoulder
as I guide you through the dark restaurants;
No more bourbon, no more twilights, no more loneliness;
no more challenging questions to your students,

no more wondering about Kafka's Penal Colony
where the great machine inscribes punishments
on the flesh of the condemned.
No more misunderstandings, rages,
memories of your depressed, suicidal sister;
dreams of your alcoholic mother
who grabs you and forces you to dance with her,
breathing in your young boy's face;
no more stories about your bullying father
who cared so much about you
he relentlessly pushed you around.

No more worries about money,
no more ex-wife, ex-house,
no more plans, no more sex,
no more thinking about sex, no more forgetting
about sex, no more anxiety about sex, no more
laughter about sex, no more memories of those girls
you wish you'd known what to do with
when they offered themselves to your hesitant touch.

No more thinking of C, arguments with C,
struggles with intimacy; no more loving nights
in the large, soft bed, your hand
reaching toward her, finding the dear bone
of her shoulder; no more wondering
how it would be to go blind.

3

You didn't want a funeral, or a memorial,
but on Sunday we gathered anyway,
not sure what we'd do or say.
It was easy to recall your wild, inspired dancing,
how you loved your kids and your students
and loathed the indecencies of our lying world.
Of course we ignored the tougher things,
kept stuff to ourselves and did a lot of laughing,
We were like a flock of small birds
unsure where to fly when those cold winds arrive.
We'd lost our radar. We couldn't read the stars.
We laughed because we were lost.

You and I had good times I wouldn't tell about
either: moments of strange delight
and mute brotherhood. And there was
your rage at me when I told you to learn braille
so you could read Kafka in your darkness.

Instead, I am learning the searing symbols of departure.
In dreams, you pack a suitcase.
I imagine seeing you, unsteady, weaving down the street.
There are hard ancient pathways inscribed in us.
Logics that address me, but I don't understand.
A language of those left behind.
It's all we have.

There was a roaring engine outside as I woke.
I lifted the blinds to discover what it was:
      —Ah! the north wind doing its late autumn work.
Gone so long,
I'd forgotten its voice.

Wild for finalities, I went out
to complete the work, grabbing
one tree after another:
first the slender witch hazel,
just my own height,
which yielded,
letting go of its last few leaves

Then a Japanese dogwood, with two narrow trunks,
about twelve feet now, the last leaves
golden brown, limbs spread eight or nine feet.
It resisted and I shook it,
shook it again and twenty or thirty leaves descended.

Then the three native dogwoods,
as high as the house, but trunks
I could almost fit my hands around—
they swayed slowly as, one by one,
their dark red leaves tumbled,
glad to let go perhaps, as
I imagined: a little push, and we're
on our brief journey.

Finally, the oak, eight feet around,
possibly eighty high. I grabbed

it nonetheless, crazed with my work
and stood there, anchored
now in the earth. As I vainly
tried to shake, I was being shaken,
hair falling from my head,
old skin swaying across my shoulders,
skeleton vibrating, the bark on me
breaking open: a bare winter man
coming forward, with uncertain eye.

I wish I could say serene,
settled in the one spot where
it was my destiny to be rooted,
but it was nothing so blessed. Instead
I became a being caught
in the downward tide
of the season—
            trembling, unknown.

        i love this thing that reminds me of you
(whatever happened, whatever was lost)

    its subtlety, the mystery in it, the slim black
metal plate it rests on

        i love the blending drenched and
imperfect colors—
            ochre, many greens, something close to yellow,
        as if the earth had been squeezed
like a sponge and this is what
dropped from it

                    every shade
            depending on the angle of the sun

        the shape curved now from use, softened,
melted into a roundness, a lip,
                    and in the center the tiny blackened remnants
        of a wick, like a nipple
on the breast of a distant planet

its fragrance is dull and sweet

        You once lit this candle and held it out to me
                    hoping
        for tender illumination.

        But the darkness we brought with us
was too great.

GHOST OF A CHANCE

The old man had the radio going.
His all night lullaby. He'd be snoring
intermittently by the time I came in
maybe 2 am, and the jazz show
on.

There was someone splashing
across the keys,
transfiguring the tune into
a swelling river
filled by innumerable creeks
where we could drink and swim.

"Willow Weep for Me" it said
or "Stardust" as I took my clothes
off, my penis sullen, delighted from hours
of petting, unable to get myself
to unbutton her blouse.
and the music dancing around me,
calling, waves of song and under
the covers my hand
quietly bringing the passionate evening
to its lonely end.

I could not know then how loneliness
itself could become a river
how there would be memory
how there would be waiting and
how the river could flow on and on
and how what mattered might

have been missed, then lost,
and how there would be
the ghost of a chance once
and never again.

ON NOT WRITING

> All birth is unwilling.
>
> —*Pearl Buck*

Captured by some crude, random associations,
and interrogated in a dark closet
as they shove me against the wall
I cannot grasp how these pieces of meaning
could seize me so powerfully
their wide glowing hands
locked against my shoulders
while I glimpse what I hope
is a forgiving look in their shadowed faces

and they want to know
why I forgot what I owe them—
the vow I made—

and, lying, I say—what vow,
when?
and they say—when you were born,
fool, countryman,

dearest brother.

> Being has not been given its due.
>
> —*Jean-Paul Sartre*

let's not
say
too much.

let's
keep
the lines
short.

there's
something
quieter

Being
needs
only
a small
space

like a
spider

legs folded

done

finally

with webs.

COUNTING

recalling my grandmother

down in the basement as the large stone
wash basin anchored to the wall was filling

with hot water, she counted to herself
as she pulled out each item in the clothes basket,

yanked it straight—a sock, undershorts,
a sheet, pillow cases, kitchen towels

and submerged it in the foaming water
and began to scrub with a fierce energy

as if something were trying to get away
and she was going to catch it

eighteen, nineteen, twenty, twenty-one.
I observed her keeping track, though she

never explained why
she needed the numbers.

And I found myself doing the same thing
as I dug up fragments of what might have been

great boulders from the ice age
in our little backyard:

Twenty, twenty-one, twenty-two
little red pebbles and flattened gray rocks;

a pile of objects to keep me company;
the numbers a kind of protest

to the god who made so many small things
and tossed them aside.

THE IGLOO

for Elizabeth

We're only a group of writers
in Jack's living room.
Outside, heavy rain turning to ice
beats on the skylight.

We take turns sitting under the lamp of truth
putting forth our words, explaining
our confusions, dressing stories
in the exquisite fog of human speech.

Some of us close our eyes, listening.
Sometimes a spark flies around the room
and burns a hole in an earlobe.
Sometimes sleep comes close
and wraps one of us
in its heavy blanket of black seal fur.

What a little tribe we are:
staring across this small space
as it grows dark, gnawing bones,
chewing the last pieces of fish flesh,
arguing over what might have happened,
what should have happened,
myths of what could have happened.
Laughing, absurdly content, knowing
we are here for the long months without
light, the world drifting as it always drifts,
among true mysteries.

> One must imagine Sisyphus happy.
>
> —*Albert Camus*

It was the fifties,
and determined to be college intellectuals,
we stayed up all night smoking French cigarettes,
listening to Bach's unaccompanied violin sonatas,
reading Camus and imagining
what Sisyphus felt.

He was proud, Belsky said.
Proud he could survive any punishment.
He was not proud, he was stuck, Roger said.
We argued. Someone asked: did Sisyphus
have a mother? Someone else asked:
did she send him salami? Was he permitted
to stop and read poetry?
Maybe he got laid every time he rolled
that rock to the top.
We were getting drunk and skeptical.

Somebody mentioned the soul.
Somebody else threw a beer bottle.
One of us went out to puke.

One day Belsky announced: "I might
kill myself . . . if I feel like it."
How? "I have pills," he said
and showed us the bottle.
Sisyphus did not kill himself,
somebody pointed out.

But Belsky had strange tendencies.
One night we pushed his door open.
He was dazed, pills
half gone, muttering "I'm a taxi
and I've turned the corner."

We dragged him out, walked him around,
scared of police, arguing through
ice caked nostril winter streets.
He slumped along, hunched over
like a wire hanger carrying too many coats.

At dawn, we pulled him up the hill
on Seventh, fed him coffee and doughnuts
and he revived, peered at us
like someone squinting through a dim microscope,

"Life is a party," he said dreamily,
"and it's still on, right?"
An exhausted Gerald spoke:
"Friend, Sisyphus just called and
wanted you to know
life is not a party."

outside i was splitting wood
oak and hickory with
a wedge and a sledgehammer,
and somehow was not able to tire myself
regardless of how frustrating it
sometimes became.

my son watched and sometimes
handed me the small ax.
he saw those pieces of sweet gum
someone had left in the woodpile
we inherited with the house,
and that, in my ignorance, i
regarded just like the other wood.
he saw however with those logs
the wood opened but did not split,
it grabbed the wedges and
hard as i hammered, would

not let them free.
he saw two wedges stuck,
one on each end of the log and
my useless, endless hammering
and asked, dad, what are we going
to do now? and i, not knowing,
ashamed to accept defeat,
looked at him, and for a moment,
lay my heavy arms down.

THE SIRENS' LATER LIVES

Even the sirens became
unbearably tired
—luring whoever happened by
with their ravishing songs.

Endless wooden ships
torn open on the rocks, endless
soul-bewildered sailors
swimming towards them,
desperate to reach this version
of the unavoidable.

Destiny, they found,
was a hideous bore.
And then too, they came to hate
the men's hands reaching up and then
vanishing under the sea.

And so, one by one, slowly
over millennia,
they chose silence.
The hypnotic voices still vibrated
in the fierce echo chambers
of their throats. But
day by day their power diminished
and they found themselves released
and strangely empty.

Then, after a while, without exactly
understanding how, they managed
to find other ways:

a murmuring amongst themselves
as they collected shells
and rocks on the beach
and they discovered
how to carve driftwood into bird shapes
and to tie their hair into fish nets
delicate as spider webs.

THE TURN

There are no courses for beginners in Life.

—Rilke

Three a.m.   after the party where he danced
      hopelessly

searching
    for her
again

stunned
    by crazy fragrances   memory

driving back on Erwin
coming to the
     turn at Whitfield
      (no one around)

accelerating into it
    swinging out

          far
veeringacross the shoulder
      arm   out the window
        breathing black
          night air
        catching
        a glimpse
          of a couple of
        clear   stars

   and he

howls

the only thing

       to do

            howls and breathes and
            leans into the night

         as the car
      steadies
    and returns
smoothly

     the pleasure
bitter and instinctive
    as if he'd learned to drive this fine line
    in a dream as if the universe
      had intended
    his thoughtless being to have this
    odd power

just as he was
    destined once to be young
    and afraid

just as   he should
        then   have trusted

the startling
    dangerous
    voice

that said:
     Don't
   let her go.

SEX

There is a difference between having a thousand experiences
and having the same experience a thousand times.

—*Mark Twain*

No one can tell exactly how it is
for you,
        but you know
                all too well.

You're finished,
sad,
        sullenly dissatisfied,
        and you get up, trying
                to be polite,
and go home.

        You turn on the engine,
and music
        blasts into the car,
and you shiver
        but don't turn it off.

It's a short trip
        home. It's a
        short trip.

PSYCHOTHERAPIST AT THE LANDFILL

for Bob Phillips

1

On an early morning in my seventy-first year
      it is a mixed thing
      to come to the county landfill
and in the piercing yellow light inter
these scribbled notes of bewilderment,
attentiveness and odd, interminable hope.

To bury them among garbage heaps
and old appliances: one hundred twenty-two
boxes of records, manilla folders
filled with my writing—
      forty years of dreams taken down
      forty years of dilemmas,
visitations from the archetypal powers,
forty years of human beings
talking out loud to themselves and to me,
pages, an unbelievable accumulation now;
evidence of how we humans struggle and ruminate,
trying against so much training,
so much fear, to dig
through the long, heavy dark and raise the dead—
      accomplish the slow, uncertain resurrection
      of becoming ourselves.

Because I could not bear to have them shredded
I now carry the boxes out
amidst the debris and dust of the landfill
and lay them here thinking somehow

they will be left alone to decay and vanish
in their own time, decompose under the stars.

Only I am wrong.
The bulldozer appears so quickly;
snorting and shoving things aside
burying the pile in efficient sweeps of its yellow plow.
       Then they're gone, pushed under—
       the fine attunements, the record of all
       I was able to make sense from—
gone into the garbage
—forty years worth in forty seconds.
Instant burial!

2

And then for a week
       I can't sleep in peace.
       I wake every morning
       and know something is wrong, unfinished.

And finally, I grasp it and go back.
I have the smudge stick with me this time
and the sage and fragrant cedar.
This time, I go up to the bulldozer,
silent, unattended now, and mark it
with my stick.
       This time, I create the fire
       and speak my makeshift
       native american/modern man
prayer:
       Commit these writings, these
       scribblings half understood, memories
       of spirit struggles, to the Great Mystery.
       May they find their place,
       a breath of our strange journey,

often obscure to us, that nonetheless,
we yearn to know.

The smoke rises and I think of the road
I have taken myself: seventy now,
retired detective of dreams.
A mixed thing to be here with prayers and endings.
My soul feels its damp exhausted
exhilaration—
        letting go of all that was healed
        and not healed—
my long initiation through the stinging
comradely sweat lodge of the years.